Grace Confounding

Grace
Confounding

Poems by
Amos Niven Wilder

Fortress Press
Philadelphia

To two old friends and associates
in a common enterprise
Stanley Romaine Hopper
Nathan A. Scott, Jr.

Table of Contents

Foreword

It is in the area of liturgics—the idiom and metaphors of prayer and witness—that a main impasse lies today for the Christian. It is hoped that these poems may help suggest the necessary mutation of categories and language.

It is at the level of the imagination that the fateful issues of our new world-experience must first be mastered. It is here that culture and history are broken, and here that the church is polarized. Old words do not reach across the new gulfs, and it is only in vision and oracle that we can chart the unknown and new-name the creatures.

Before the message there must be the vision, before the sermon the hymn, before the prose the poem.

.   .   .   .

Before any new theologies however secular and radical there must be a contemporary theo-poetic. The structures of faith and confession have always rested on hierophanies and images. But in each new age and climate the theo-poetic of the church is reshaped in inseparable relation to the general imagination of the time.

Any such new theo-poetic or world-dramatization is also old. It links the revelations of the past with disclosures in the present. It weds ancient myth with our own actuality. A contemporary witness identifies itself with our modern mythologies even the most ambiguous, both exploiting and purging them.

.   .   .   .

Old words do not reach across the new gulfs. We can therefore understand the disarray in the churches and the exodus of the disaffected. But it is not as though the old words, hymns, confessions, oratorios have not been true in their own setting. They are still true and valid. It is not as though God were dead and the world with no

plan. Christ is still risen indeed. It is still true that the
multitude of all the peoples that fight against Ariel—Zion
—shall be as a dream of a night vision. The ancient cov-
enant morticed in the foundations of the world still holds.
But these realities have to be seen, heard, felt as true
where we are and in our own vernacular. These appre-
hensions have to come to life in our own theatre of
experience. The terms of our Christian eloquence have to
be relocated. Our liturgies should reflect this, and all the
media and gestures of prayer, witness and deed. Again
it is hoped that certain of these poems may suggest this
kind of mutation of speech. Does not the New Testament
itself promise new tongues, new names, new songs?

.   .   .   .

But what of Christian action? Is not the real impasse
of the Gospel today to be found at the point of the
deed rather than at that of language and images? If our
theo-poetic is only a superficially aesthetic matter this
objection is unanswerable. But there is no potent and
undiscouragable deed without passion, and no passion
without imagination. Christian mission in our contem-
porary theatre of action requires—both for orientation and
for power—a liturgy and a theo-poetic whose language
speaks for the modern sensibility.

A Christian doxology today can see the power of the
Resurrection shattering not the stones of an ancient
burial niche but the vanadium vaults of modern acquisi-
tiveness and the massive legalities which sanction and
bulwark our inhumanities. The principalities and powers
that preside over our global disorders are undermined and
our obsessions dispelled by the same elder Charity which
was from the beginning. Ever and again the Kingdom
comes in new occasions and the zeal of the Lord of
Sabaoth can vaporize the indurated strongholds of mod-
ern power. On the right hand and on the left, against all
expectations, righteousness appears from nowhere, like
dew. All such endowments and tasks and their contem-

porary strategies find their voice in new litanies, hymns, folksongs and proclamations.

It is in the magnetic field of the Spirit, between the poles of present need and grace, that faith remints its language, merging old vision with new and combining archaic legacies with leadings of today and tomorrow. Our modern experience requires its own categories, genres, idioms not only to achieve communication today, and not only to enable its own arts and celebrations, but also so that the scriptures of the past may have a voice to speak to us anew.

. . . .

I would be the first to recognize that these poems represent only one kind of new idiom. Many of them indeed depart very little from traditional patterns. Other more revolutionary styles are to be welcomed in all aspects of Christian celebration. The trend in various religious circles today toward new media in liturgy and communication properly follows various strategies. The spirits are always to be tested but the Spirit is never to be quenched. It is not always easy in a time like ours to apply a theological test to the more iconoclastic modes and vehicles but discrimination can at least require a highly disciplined artistic competence. Creative improvisation is wholly compatible with traditional mastery and indeed demands it. Beyond this test the long history of Christian worship and enthusiasm has sufficiently forewarned us against various masquerades of sub-Christian impulse and myths of innocence.

These poems may be seen as the pursuit in another genre of my work as a student of the New Testament, and as one specially concerned with its modes of language. I have always urged on my colleagues due recognition of the plastic and metaphorical aspects of the Scriptures and the relation of the Word of God to the changing rhetorics of time and place. The poems also reflect my long concern as a theologian with modern letters and the resources that Christian praise and witness may find in our encounter with modern secular experience and its arts. The dedication of the book to Stanley Romaine Hopper and Nathan A. Scott, Jr. has thus its appropriateness.

Since here, however, it is particularly a question of poetry I would like also to pay my tribute to two teachers, Charles H. A. Wager of Oberlin, and William Lyon Phelps of Yale; also to two poets, Kenneth Patchen and Eric Schroeder, who long ago initiated me into the work of Eliot, Hart Crane and other "modern" poets; to Herbert Hitchen, Earl Marlatt, Arnold Kenseth and John Holmes whose names evoke earlier associations in the New England Poetry Society; and finally three more closely related: my sister Charlotte Wilder who (with Ben Belitt) won the Shelley Memorial Award in poetry in 1939, my mother who was translating poets like Carducci and Verhaeren when we were children, and my wife, Catharine, who apart from other inestimable benefits always unreservedly furthered and safeguarded these literary pursuits amid other claims of the family, and who helped to shape the present collection.

A.N.W.

Acknowledgments

Grateful acknowledgment is made to the following publishers and journals for permission to re-print in this volume poems which have previously appeared:

To Yale University Press, New Haven, Connecticut, publishers in 1928 of *Arachne: Poems* for "Transmigration," "So Is It," "Shakespeare to the Friend in the Sonnets," "Logos," and "The New Aphrodite."

To Harper & Row, New York, New York, publishers in 1943 of *The Healing of the Waters* for "The City of Destruction," "Doom," "Unshriven," "To the God of Deliverances," "To Pulpit and Tribune," "This Day," "Homage," "Prayer Without Words," "Alive for Evermore," "The Eternal Patience," and "November Dusk." (© 1943 by Harper & Brothers).

To *The Christian Century*, Chicago, Illinois for "Grace Confounding" (© 1963 by the Christian Century Foundation), "The Nativity" (here titled "The Play Within the Play") (© 1965 by the Christian Century Foundation), "The Third Day" (© 1965 by the Christian Century Foundation), "The Journey of the Magi" (© 1967 by the Christian Century Foundation), and "Electric Chimes or Rams' Horns" (© 1971 by the Christian Century Foundation).

To *Christianity and Crisis*, New York, New York, for "An Old Family Argument" (originally entitled "Dialogue at Christmas") and "Discord and Resolution."

To *Poetry*, Chicago, Illinois, which has released the copyright to "A Hard Death."

To *The Christian Scholar* (now *Soundings*), New Haven, Connecticut, for "The Ancient Pattern," a translation of *Lebenslauf* by Hölderlin.

To Carl Winter—Universitätsverlag, Heidelberg for "Autumn Fires" (a translation from Hölderlin) and "The Twice-Born" (after Rilke), both of which appeared in *Festschrift zum 75 Geburtstag von Theodor Spira*, herausgegeben von H. Viebroch und W. Erzgräber, 1961.

Grace Confounding

Grace Confounding

He came when he wasn't expected
as He always does,
though a few on the night-shift had the release early.

He came where he wasn't expected
as He always does,
though a few mages were tipped off.

He came where even the Apostles couldn't go along,
in Nazareth of all places, on the edge of nowhere;
they had to place it in David's home town.

He is always one step ahead of us;
the space-age calls for new maps
and its altars and holy places are not yet marked.

This Day

*This day is a day of trouble, and of rebuke, and of
contumely; for the children are come to the birth, and
there is not strength to bring forth. (Isaiah 37:3)*

*Shall I bring to the birth, and not cause to bring forth?
saith the Lord. (Isaiah 66:9)*

As though our world had never seen the thorn
Bear at long last the unimagined rose,
And we ourselves had never seen the morn
After a night of storm its pomps unclose;

As though no selfsame testimony ran
From clan to empire and from clime to clime:
"The inscrutable gods pursue their cryptic plan,
An unthought fabric pays the cost of time;

Some undreamed crystal marks the ancient throes,
Some breathless temple stands above the tide,
Some arch of peace atones a myriad woes,
Some coral ridge stands when the seas subside."

O wait upon the ancient miracle
Ever renewed, seize the eventual boon.
Feel through these years some tide of purpose swell
Otherwise great, now in the world's mid-noon.

These infinite tasks are portents of a Work
Afoot among us toward transcendent ends;
Behind these ruins and these hungers lurk
Strategies unsurmised and secret trends.

. . . .

Hast thou not known and heard? For He who made
The earth, and not in vain, by his dispose
Unsearchable here also undismayed
Triumphs, and ever best found in the close.

The Third Day

The immovable stone tossed aside,
The collapsed linens,
The blinding angel and the chalky guards:
All today like an old wood-cut.

The earthquake on the third day,
The awakened sleeper,
The ubiquitous stranger, gardener, fisherman:
Faded frescoes from a buried world.

Retell, renew the event
In these planetary years,
For we were there and He is here:
It is always the third day.

Our world-prison is split;
An elder charity
Breaks through these modern fates.
Publish it by Telstar,
Diffuse it by mundovision.

He passes through the shattered concrete slabs,
The vaporized vanadium vaults,
The twisted barbed-wire trestles.

A charity coeval with the suns
Dispels the deep obsessions of the age
And opens heart-room in our sterile dream:
A new space within space to celebrate
With mobiles and new choreographies,
A new time within time to set to music.

An Old Family Argument

One of the *minim* burst in on the Rabbi and exclaimed:
  "The Messiah has come!"
The Rabbi went to the window and looked out,
    and demurred:
  "Nothing has changed.

"As of old,
Seedtime and harvest, cold and heat, day and night:
A generation goes and a generation comes
But the earth remaineth the same.
What is crooked is not made straight.

"As of old,
A time to weep and a time to laugh,
A time to mourn and a time to dance,
A time to love and a time to hate,
A time for war and a time for peace;
There is nothing new under the sun.
The King tarrieth.
What is wanting is not made up."

NEVERTHELESS, the Kingdom has come;
Behind the scenes, a clandestine irruption;
A fission in the world's grain,
A benign conflagration.
O Lord, open the eyes of thy servants:
Behold, the mountain full of horses and chariots of fire.

Nothing has changed? But listen:
Tellurian tremors,
Convulsions at the earth's core,
The silent collapse of parapets.
Moorings have parted
And we are carried into new latitudes.

The Kingdom cometh not with observation,
But it has overtaken us
Dispelling old obsessions.

Therefore this dancing through iron doors,
This singing our way through blind walls,
This mocking of old hierarchic dooms,
Levitation across impassable wastes.

Therefore these hilarities, against all reason,
And charities welling up for no cause.
Righteousness appears from nowhere, like dew,
The earth opens and joy springs in the furrows
And the angels acclaim it from pole to pole.

Discord and Resolution

Von wegen geringer Dinge
Verstimmt wie vom Schnee war
Die Glocke, womit
Man läutet
Zum Abendessen.
          Hölderlin, "Entwurf zu Kolomb"

As in a snowfall
the vesper bells
that call men from the fields
to the evening meal
come dissonant and muted,
their changes
jumbled in the swarming dusk;

as through a swirling fog
the dead clangs of the bell-buoy
swinging to the surges
reach us muffled and awry,
deranged in the smother;

so the tolling of being
is damped and untuned,
the chime of creation
and the diapason of the heart
jangled by a swarm,
a fate, of lesser things,
or, as in the Seventh Circle,
by Dante's slow rain
of fiery flakes,

until by some hurtless ban
that old world-weather clears
and that old encroachment is dispelled
and we hear again the clamor of the angelic choirs
on true pitch
and their well-tempered accords,
as when the morning stars sang together
and all the sons of God shouted for joy.

The Journey of the Magi

Heirs of a lost dominion
and fallen from far
we grope our way
bemused in alien systems,
our primogeniture forgotten.

Following the star
we move through sleep-walking throngs,
the heartless ballet
of cyphers and series,
towards human climates;

moving from these simulacra
to form;
from this world-clock
and iron spell,
this stuttering on an obsessive note,
to song;
from this thinning bell-jar,
from vacuum and vertigo,
to a field of force
crackling,
to joy.

The star moves on above burning villages and suburbs,
higher than floating flares and rockets,
and outshines our satellites and blast-offs

toward this wattled crib
and these cast-offs in the byre,
this lowly, holy, this infinitely gentle sign
that shall rebuke our distemper
and dispel our haggardie
and make all our devisings benign.

Doom
After Isaiah

The age is febrile and beside itself:
Ridden by ten thousand passions, unawares
Fallen on alienation; 'tis a house
By seven disastrous demons dispossessed
Who hold unreckoning carnival and trade
In dyes and linens and the souls of men.
The generation is adulterous:
Its vows abjured in hoarse rapacity,
Its faiths all sponged in truculent despair.
It runs on heartless courses, and pursues
Insensate quests and strange obsessive cares.
This people is accursed and knoweth not
The law, but plunged in brazen cecity
Calls peace what is not peace and darkness light,
Shouts on the housetops while the parapets
Crumble and fall before the battering rams.
Too soon the chariots roar about the streets,
Too soon the incendiaries fly like fiends
With torches in the alley-ways. Alas!
The palaces, the ivory summer houses,
The cedar work and gay partitions blaze;
And of the temple stones that housed the Presence
No longer one upon the other left.

Electric Chimes or Rams' Horns

*The following advertisement in support of church attendance was published in a magazine of national circulation.**

"Sure you vote, pay taxes, work hard, make money, and have made out a will. But you must do something more to become a first-class citizen. You must experience the benefits that come from going to church regularly. Your children will respect you more. Your neighbor will look up not just across to you. Your community will recognize you as a participant, not just a passer-by. Your country will be stronger, for you will enforce that spiritual fabric so essential to its continuing welfare. But the person who will benefit most is you. You will get the stimulation and reward of understanding the brotherhood of man, the dignity that the individual can derive from worship. You will equip yourself to cope with all the complications that eternally face us all. You will make the other 167 hours each week truly worth living. See for yourself—next Sunday."

Yes, go to church next Sunday,
take time out on Vanity Fair,
enter into the hurricane eye
while the winds blow outside.
But don't leave the world behind you,
take it in with you:
after all, it was here with God's word
that it was all set in motion.

"Take your family to church next Sunday."
(Compel them to come in." Luke 14:23)
No, better just tell them where you are going,
remember that generation gap.

* *The Reader's Digest*, vol.77, no.459 (July 1960), p.2. By permission.

Join the parade on Fifth Avenue or Main Street.
Rather, join the ancient procession through the
  wilderness,
the trek as old as Abraham.
Fall in with the tribes that moved through the desert
and knew the scorpions and the manna.
Elbow the shadows in the catacombs
and those who gathered in the Cevennes,
the proscribed and the harried of all lands,
with the stigma of the Cross or the star of David,
or the armband of the resistance.
Company with the pilgrims of all times.
Hear the sound not of the new electric chimes
but of the ancient rams' horns.

Yes, "go to church on Sunday,"
but why not also on some other day when there is
  no one there?
Or on some week night when there is a church
  meeting:
perhaps you can help change the hymn book
  or get rid of that chromo by Hofmann,
or help vote the church into a merger and out of
  existence into a larger life.
And don't think too much of that dignity
or sink too far into the foam-rubber seats or the
  organ tremolo.

Go up to Zion: hear the angels sing and look through
  the trapdoor into Abaddon.
Go through the door not only with the Smiths
  and the Jones,
with the garage man and the banker,
but with David and Isaiah, Peter and Thomas,
  Mary and Martha.
Kneel not only with your neighbors, benign
  or distracted,

but with Hagar and Job, Anna and Stephen;
yes, with Jephthah's daughter, immolated for a vow
    (she is still with us),
and with Rizpah whose sons were impaled as an
expiation (she may be sitting next to you),
with the Magdalen and Ananias and Judas.

Look on the Seven Lamps of the Apocalypse
and consider the guttering torches of time.
See where the flickering candle flares and drips,
Fly the immense eclipse.
Go not to be tranquillized
but to be exorcised.

Yes, go to church and to Mt. Zion,
to the assembly of the first-born
and an innumerable company of angels,
keeping holiday with songs—but with fear
    and trembling.
Draw near to the holy mountain
as to Sinai enveloped in smoke
with its tremors and flowing lava.
Behind the familiar eleven o'clock exercises
are ancient congregations and glories,
voices and paeans and chariots of fire,
and a great white throne.

To draw near is to take your life in your hand.
Going to church is like approaching an open volcano
where the world is molten
and hearts are sifted.
The altar is like a third rail that spatters sparks,
the sanctuary is like the chamber next the
    atomic oven:
there are invisible rays and you leave your
    watch outside.

Go, therefore, not to be tranquilized
but to be exorcised.
Follow the pillar of fire and the pillar of cloud
with exultation and abandon,
with fear and trembling,
for the zeal of the Lord of Hosts
whether in the streets or the council chamber,
whether in the school or the sanctuary
waits not on the circumspect
and the flames of love
both bless and consume.

The City of Destruction

Paris, Boulevard de Clichy, August 1939

And the men of the city said unto Elisha, Behold, we
pray thee, the situation of this city is pleasant, as
my lord seeth: but the water is bad, and the land
miscarrieth. (II Kings 2:19)

And there came two angels to Sodom at even. . . . And
they said, Nay; but we will abide in the street all
night. (Genesis 19:1,2)

They did eat, they drank, they bought, they sold,
they planted, they builded; But the same day that
Lot went out of Sodom it rained fire and brimstone
from heaven, and destroyed them all. (Luke 17:28,29)

       The vision of the streets,
       The vision of the city,
       The vision of the generations:

       One city, all cities,
       Babylon, Tyre,
       Jerusalem, Rome,
       The city of man,
       The City of Destruction.

          .   .   .   .

       They throng on the boulevards,
       They press by the tables,
       They overflow on the pavement,
       They loiter, they assemble, they pass.
       The surges advance and are broken.
       The multitude drifts,
       The welter of waves has no end:
       This stream of this gulf of the ocean of man.

From center and faubourg,
From every quarter,
Both young and old
Take their place in the concourse,
Issue from by-streets,
Emerge from the Métro.
They teem at the corners,
They weave and they mill.

They spy out diversions
And gloat upon rumor,
And gather in knots
Where voices are raised,
Where mischance befalls,
Where mischief is mooted,
Where heads may be broken,
Where blood may be drawn.

They compass about
The kiosks and the stalls,
The purveyors of news,
The criers of ill-tidings,
Alarm, defamation,
The tribunes of slander,
The fliers of faction,
The banners of schism.

They mass at the doors
Of the temples of chance,
The lottery booths,
They kneel at the rail,
They commune at the comptoir,
They snatch at the lots
And fight for the numbers,
They elbow their way
To the racing affiches,
And devour the dispatches.

They stream in and out
Of the cinema caves
Where a phantasmagoria
Is cast on the night;
Where, bloodless and jaded,
They borrow of life
From flickers and fictions;
Where echoes of passion
And shadows of impulse
Move in their minds;
Where hammered by violence,
Needled by sadism,
Scalded by pungencies,
The illusion of power
Flatters their nullity;
By galvanic shocks
Convulsed for an hour;
By spectral transfusions
Alive for a season.

They pass down the by-ways
Where street-lamps are dimmed
And the house-fronts are blind,
The notorious quarter.
Bolts slide in their grooves,
Doors shut and are opened,
There are rustlings in portals,
Procurers at corners,
Invitations in whispers,
Provocations in shadows,
Perfumes and sorcery.
These are her mazes,
The concession of Astarte,
Where Circe spreads her banquets,
And love flaunts her arcana,
Where the soul is aspired
In the pit of the senses,
The funnel of Hell.

They compass about
The wrestlers, the clowns,
Marionettes
About marionettes;
Scenting out scandal,
Avid for victims,
Famished for calumny,
Fainting for blood.

   .   .   .   .

The watchman on the roof,
His clarion mocked;
The prophet in the bazaar,
Reviled by the doomed;
The angel in the street,
Jostled by the damned.

   .   .   .   .

For they beckon destruction,
They draw the avenger
With cart ropes and cords,
Defying the Furies,
Deriding disaster;
A city insensate,
They shout on the housetops,
They sit down to drink
And rise up to play,
Their hearts overcharged
With banqueting, surfeiting,
They curse in the alleys,
They reel in the gardens,
They say, Let us see it!
Ay, let it draw nigh!

And the foe asks no better,
His hordes are in motion,
The archers are prompt,
The horsemen are instant,
The chariots thunder.

The city has summoned
The ram and the mortar,
The fiery shafts,
The swordsman, the headsman,
The horrible rector.

And the Lord said,
The cry of the city is great,
I will go down now and see.

And I stood in the garish streets at nightfall
In the last days of the city
While the earth trembled
And the air grew sulphurous
And convolutions of livid smoke boiled up from the
    neighboring crater;
Electric tensions played
And a strange glare lighted the faces of the living dead.
I passed through the Carnival,
Jostled by the masquers,
And I heard the execrations and the blasphemies.

And I halted where the ways cross
Facing the oncoming throng,
Memorizing and devouring those faces and those forms
As Dante and Vergil halted in Malebolge
Confronting the scourged torrents of the damned,
And like them I beheld malice wedded with woe,
For judgment foreruns judgment
And destruction sends out its angels before.
For here were new forms of penalty,
Unsuspected plagues and new fashions in anguish,
New engines and demonries,
And new imaginations in dolor;
And the tormented were the tormenters,
And the harriers the harried,
Sinned against and sinning,
And the victims were the guilty.

And I saw the streaming throngs of the city,
Infected, riddled, pocked and blistered—
A basket of figs, very bad, so bad they cannot be eaten—
A people with fatal legacies,
A race with a fatal inheritance,
A cloth eaten by acids,
Charred by withering fires;
And all these souls agonized as men are agonized
By forethought and afterthought,
The review and the anticipation,
Stretched in a torture chamber of solicitude,
In the exquisite torments of conscience
Where imagination raises all to the infinite scale.

And in that circle whence, if report be true,
None ever return alive,
I saw familiar forms
And recognized ancient offenders;
Branded as aforetime, and with the well-known insignia,
And the tell-tale gait and gestures,
Themselves and their progeny:
All indeed the sons of Adam, with his harrowing visage,
With the image of God in eclipse, and the countenance
     darkened,
But darkened diversely,
And the daughters of Eve with her troubled demeanor,
But troubled diversely.
Thus, Cain with his brand and his sentence,
Solitary in the concourse of his brethren,
And at bay amid the indifferent.
And Ishmael, hating and hated, for every man's hand is
     against him.
And the builders of Babel, the crass, untaught by their
     ancient effrontery,
Avid and febrile still to pile up storey on storey
And show themselves insolent against the Almighty.

And Potiphar's wife and her kind, idle, unyoked,
    disencumbered,
The wanton daughters of Zion that walk with
    mincing steps,
Their vacant hours given to the arts and rites of
    their beauty:
Unguents from the perfumer and kohl at the apothecary.
At home they pore upon mirrors and glance aside
    into fountains,
Fretful and gnawed by dalliance.
They linger at the doors, they twitch the curtains,
    they sigh at the casements.
I have decked my bed, saith she, with coverings
    of tapestry and fine linen from Egypt,
I have perfumed my bed with myrrh, aloes and cinnamon,
For the goodman is not at home, he is gone a long journey.

And I saw the wretched son of Shimei who goes cursing,
Unconscious of the throng, pale, and muttering with
    paranoid intensity,
Who holds to life by this, whose ecstacy is his hate,
And whose song is his malediction.
How opened for him these poisoned wells?
And where runs the network of these channels of venom?

And I saw the dwarf of covetousness,
With the scorched soul and the febrile pulse;
He betrays himself in his ways: he is so conscious of the
    one thing he is unconscious of all else,
And unwittingly he presents himself as the fool.
So often and so long has he pored on the images
    of chance,
Gloated on the images of aggrandizement,
That he is less now a man than a lust.
He is a dedicated spirit as devils are dedicated,
And so dedicated that he has offered up father and
    mother, brother and sister, wife and child, sunlight
    and starlight.

And I saw again the warped ghost with the
    lascivious squint,
Hawking the ways and conveying his solicitations,
Beating the thickets for his game,
Adept in appraisal,
Pastmaster in the sleights and cues of his commerce.
He moves enveloped in the images of lust
And feeding on the secret hoard of lubricity,
And his eyes are full of adultery.
This plague is more instant and consuming than those
    of the body, though it goes before them.
Here man's nature is uncreated from of old.

I saw moreover the reluctant and surprised child of
    wrath that had betrayed the woman
And stumbled on inklings of that wherewith he had to do;
For out of fatality the soul speaks,
And in the hour of treachery as in the hour of death
    the innocent are august;
And he goes with eyes darkened and a brand on his brow,
And a sound of terror in his ears.

And I saw the insensate and fatuous mother
Who not only stood in the fire but led her youngest
    children with her;
And the unweaned babe with the mystery still on its face
Wheeled at night through the infernal streets
Where the fiery flakes of malediction whip the
    recalcitrant and drive them to fury.

  So the glare of the Pit played on the city,
  Its fissures open in the streets,
  Its fumes frenzy the multitude,
  Its lavas rise in the heart
  And its particles lacerate the flesh.

The oracle of the streets,
The oracle of the city,
Nineveh, Babylon, Tyre;
One city, all cities,
The Cities of the Plain,
The city of man:

Up, get you out!
Escape for your life,
Look not behind,
Neither stay in the plain,
Flee to the mountains
Lest you be consumed,

When the earth opens up
And engulfs the blasphemers,
When sulphur and brimstone
Rain from the skies,
When the windows of heaven
Are opened and the living
Are whelmed in the waters
And choked in the deluge.

O Lord, cast a branch into these fountains that they
     be sweetened.
Cast salt into these springs and heal these waters
For the water is bad and the land miscarrieth;
Let there not be from thence any more death
     or miscarrying.
O Lord, sterilize these ancient roots of ill;
Quench these perennial fires.
Allay these coursing fevers,
And bring us from these transports into thy peace.

Ariel! Lion of God!—
The Church in New Times

And the multitude of all the nations that fight against
Ariel shall be as a dream of a night vision. (Isaiah 29:7)

Through time and times
to the new generations,
new cities and migrations,
down to this latest hour
declare,
watchman upon your tower,
the apparition of Zion;
that City hail:
Ariel! Ariel!
"Lion of God" where David was encamped,
see where its lightnings flare.

Still as in times gone by
when none could unriddle the dream
or give the interpretation
now in this later age
Lion of Judah, stem
of David, open the scroll,
blazon the eternal Zion.
Still in our generation,
prophet and sage,
break open once again the seven seals.

For the new tribes and nations,
oncoming multitudes
bemused in ancient spells,
strike water from the rock
in these new latitudes;
delve, shepherd of the flock,
open the ancient wells.

Now in new generations,
new sieges, occupations,
beleaguered prophet, rise,
bid the young men lift up their eyes:
around the invested city burn
horses and chariots of fire.

Turn,
prisoners of hope, harried and driven,
turn to the stronghold when the trumpet calls,
the fortified city and the brazen walls;
God's arrows shall go forth like levin.

New Babylons melt and form
like clouds, and in new climes
new tribes and myriads swarm;
still to these foundering Tyres
and darkened lands
still in these latest times
proclaim
a glorious throne
set up on high,
our sanctuary;
acclaim
that stone
cut from the mountain without hands,
against the idols hurled,
that breaks in pieces adamant and clay
and in our latter day
grows to a mountain that shall fill the world.

The Play Within the Play

"the play within a play
Consumes the play and all the world . . ."
Henry Rago, "In that Fierce Country"

The play within the play resolves the whole:
Five acts of Hamlet focused in one scene;
It lights up one and all,
What shall be, what has been.

The play within the play! The obscure transaction
Of Advent in time's pageants new and old
Gathers the ages in one action,
The thoughts of many hearts revealed.

The play within the play: the Birth, the sequel;
This masque consumes old Adam's proud charade
From Alpha to Omega;
This hidden plot, this fuse well laid.

"What means this play?" the usurper cries distraught
From age to age. "Lights! Lights! Break off the mime!"
The conscience of the king is caught,
His proud millenial kingdom undermined.

The incognito that steps upon the stage,
The zeal that was from the beginning, shrives
The world's great rage,
The carnival of time.

A Hard Death

*"God is hidden in all the veils of evil in
order that he may overcome them all."* Martin Luther

*Right dear in the sight of the Lord
is the death of his saints:*
the death—and the dying,
and even, yes, death in such wise
in long hours of extenuation
at the uttermost ebb.

Right dear in his sight:
maintain, maintain this scandal
and be instructed by unreason.
The ruin in nature
proffers auguries.

In our sight the protracted throes,
the trances of dissolution,
the passage through the rough jaws,
the lot and necessity of the mortal
that was and is and is not.
The grass withereth, the flower fadeth.

In our sight the torn fibres
and sunderings,
dread at the brink
and stupor at the unknown,
creaturely
benightedness of the living.

In our sight, law
mindless and immitigable,
the machinery of the natural cycle.
O lion limb against me,
insensate stifler.
Accept no mitigation
but be instructed at the null point:
the zero
breeds new algebras.

Warp of the loom,
death waits not on dying
but conspires with both our ripeness
and our taking-off;
colors the flower
as it wastes the fruit.
Nescience is in our knowing
as eternity in the heart.

Accept no mitigation,
refuse all sleek ensolacings:
the harshest mother is the most fecund.
A savage assuagement cries
with a savage voice.

The null point
breeds new algebras,
the ruin in nature
proffers auguries.
This hammer
strikes sparks from the heart,
the double-axe has its fulgurations.

Death like a dam
arouses the deep;
off the Big Sur the shoals
surprise the currents of the main.
The hidden ledge
turns turquoise into snow,
and phosphorescence
burns round the granite reef.

Alien: A Period Piece

I found the gates of beauty barred,
   I heard the strains within;
A hireling in the outer yard
   Thereto I could not win;
With members scarred and visage marred
   How should I enter in?

Those pomps of pageantry and song,
   Those wide demesnes of grace,
To other happier lots belong,
   A more felicitous race;
My hurt would wrong that blissful throng
   And cloud that lambent place.

A pilgrim over shards and sands
   I heard those staves of joy
Fitfully blown from fabled lands
   Strangers to our annoy
Where love's commands give whiter hands
   More musical employ.

I found the bolts of beauty drawn
   Against the wounds and dust
Of bondage, but a carillon
   Within blew like a gust
Of fragrance from an incensed dawn
   Holier than our lust.

I found the bars of beauty up,
   Her watchers on the wall;
Within those courts I might not sup
   Nor tarry there at all;
But where they supped with bread and cup
   I hailed their festival.

Dante and Beatrice at the Ponte della Trini

This was no chance encounter, since we both
Had felt the still disturbance of the soul,
The shock of mutual awe and mystic troth.

As gong wakes gong, and when long tremors roll
From ocean far abandoned belfries toll,
So rang our hearts and spoke their silent oath.

Hölderlin, "Reif sind, in Feuer getaucht"

Reif sind, in Feuer getaucht, gekochet
Die Frücht und auf der Erde geprüfet, und ein Gesetz ist,
Dass alles hineingeht, Schlangen gleich,
Prophetisch, träumend auf
Den Hügeln des Himmels. Und vieles
Wie auf den Schultern eine
Last von Scheitern, ist
Zu behalten. Aber bös sind
Die Pfade. Nämlich unrecht,
Wie Rosse, gehn die gefangenen
Element und alten
Gesetze der Erd. Und immer
Ins Ungebundene gehet eine Sehnsucht. Vieles aber ist
Zu behalten. Und not die Treue.
Vorwärts aber und rückwärts wollen wir
Nicht sehn. Uns wiegen lassen, wie
Auf schwankem Kahne der See.

Autumn Fires
A Translation from Hölderlin

Ripe is the harvest
seared in the blaze of summer,
and the fruits of the earth
baptized and proven with fire;
and it is a law
that all should pass through the flames
like salamanders, prophetic
and dreaming of the high hills of heaven.
Yet much abides and is cherished,
a burden of fragments from our ruins.
But evil are the ways, and ruthlessly
the ancient and unalterable laws of the earth
plod like stallions;
and a longing arises continually
towards that which is beyond our Necessity.
Yet much abides and is cherished,
and one thing is needful, our fidelity.
Before and after let us not look,
but rather as in a fragile craft
be rocked on the sea.

Hölderlin, Lebenslauf
(Erweiterte Fassung)

Grössres wolltest auch du, aber die Liebe zwingt
  All uns nieder, das Leid beuget gewaltiger,
    Doch es kehret umsonst nicht
      Unser Bogen, woher er kommt.

Aufwärts oder hinab! wehet in heilger Nacht,
  Wo die stumme Natur werdende Tage sinnt,
    Weht im nüchternen Orkus
      Nicht ein liebender Atem auch?

Dies erfuhr ich. Doch nie, sterblichen Meistern gleich,
  Habt ihr Himmlichen, ihr Alleserhaltenden,
    Dass ich wüsste, mit Vorsicht
      Mich des ebenen Pfads geführt.

Alles prüfe der Mensch, sagen die Himmlischen,
  Dass er, kräftig genährt, danken für alles lern,
    Und verstehe die Freiheit,
      Aufzubrechen, wohin er will.

The Ancient Pattern
Hölderlin's "Lebenslauf"

You, too, aspired after greater things
But love and its earthly bonds and the law of the creature
Proclaimed their ancient rights,
And duress bows us down with irresistible force.

The rainbow returns to the earth from which it arose
But it is not in vain or without meaning.

Whether we soar or fall, a divine justice presides
Whether in the womb of the unborn
Or in deepest Orcus.

This I have learned.
For you, O heavenly powers that maintain all that is,
You, as I well know, have never led me by smooth paths
As did my mortal masters.

Let man prove all things—say the heavenly ones—
So that he may be mightily nurtured,
And learn to render thanks for all;
And, whatever his own course,
Be taught, notwithstanding, to hail the dawn of freedom.

Rilke, "*Siehe, ich wusste es sind*"

Siehe, ich wusste es sind
solche, die nie den gemeinsamen Gang
lernten zwischen den Menschen . . .

Eh sie noch lächelten
weinten sie schon vor Freude;
eh sie noch weinten
war die Freude schon ewig . . .

Eines ist Schicksal. Da werden die Menschen
sichtbarer. Stehn wie Türme. Verfalln.
Aber die Liebenden gehn
über der eignen Zerstörung
ewig hervor; denn aus dem Ewigen
ist kein Ausweg. Wer widerruft
Jubel?

Gedichte für Lulu Albert-Lazard, VII.

The Twice-Born
After Rilke: "Siehe, ich wusste . . ."

From the first
as with lovers
their felicity is full-blown,
as though a membrane burst
and joy had giant grown.
From the initial surprise
and instant enthralment
their glory is already endless.
And as with lovers
the human tears of joy
come after,
and later still the human laughter.
Where fate rules and accident
the lot of men is known;
like towers they stand, they fall.
But for the blest, beyond
their proper dissolution,
they soar forever and forever
past all recall.
From such foreordination
swerving there is none.
Such canticles
who annuls?

Transmigration

We pass through worlds and worlds in sleep;
The pilgrim in the lowly inn
Bears no trace of the mighty deep
Nor of the spheres where he has been.
We pass through Limbos, and forget;
Impoverished of our shadowy lore
Of principalities that yet
Glimmer, and powers we sense no more.
For no substantial being is ours.
We glass the deep abysses blind,
And there the flare of Tophet lowers
Where late the Seven Candles shined.
We traverse suns and moons in sleep
And guard no records of the deep.

Shakespeare
to the Friend in the Sonnets

The scythes of time play havoc with the swarms
That breed and sicken on our dying globe
And shadowy harvests of unnumbered forms
Fall to the ruthless shafts that search and probe;
The circling moons put in their silvery flail,
Earth's gibbering phantoms flutter to the shade;
At last the moon's own lustrous course shall fail
And cinders strew the track the Pleiads made.
But thy dream-molded face shall haunt the gods
Embalmed in pity in the eternal thought,
And leap oblivion in those high abodes
To live anew in Edens newly wrought.
Then from this closing dark, O lighted face,
Bear record of me to that shining place.

The Birth of Joy

I do not believe this
but I waive that denial,
I do not believe this
(too well I know,
too often . . .)
but I ban that knowledge,
I suffer the sweet persuasion,
I avert my eyes.
This moment is just as real, deny its succession.

Let joy be,
chill it not,
give it room,
against hope admit it this space,
suffer it thus far.
Who knows?
Such virtue it has
it might usurp even upon this desolation,
reclaim even these ruins upon ruins
and conjure away out of all worlds
this voice that denies.

You cannot conceive how foolish
these presumptions of joy,
what vagaries of fancy,
what conceits,
what untrammeled conceits overleaping all reason,
mocking every certainty.

This is the music of the heart that has its own space,
its own firmaments and freedom.

From so precarious, so absurd a station,
this foothold on make-believe,
it launches out,
fills its own space
with dizzy and endless exfoliations,
builds its own insubstantial architecture,
and leaving in oblivion that first fiction
inhabits its own adamantine order.

November Dusk
College Hill, Hamilton College

The forests leaned and tossed and swayed,
The paths were matted with the leaves,—
But that tumultuous dusk bereaved
My heart of ill and dread.

The darkness drifted through the boughs
And overhead the still cloud raced,
And I recalled another place
And other vows.

The breath of some resistless might
Was in the pines, and their deep chant
Sang to the soul that powers haunt
The earth on such a night.

The leaves sustained their frenzied dance,
The crows fled on the flood of wind,—
And I was deaf and I was blind
In that dread circumstance.

For as the pines, my chords were thrilled,
And as the crows, my flight was borne,
And as the earth, my heights were stormed,
My heaven filled.

What mighty Pan was at his task?
What awful voice had spoken there?
His naked arm I saw him bare,
I saw the god unmask.

Vita Nuova

The celebrated bas-relief in the Museo delle
Terme at Rome, often called "The Birth of Venus,"
represents the rise of an initiate from an
immersion effecting immortality in one of the
mystery cults.

A new soul in an empyrean new
Clasped by old loves renewed! from the shared Passion
Of Attis stricken in a world grown ashen
To waken in a world new washed with dew,
All forms grown lovelier and every hue
More lively, and to look upon the fashion
Of stainless firmaments and the compassion
Of wondrous beings such as childhood knew.
O from this haunted sleep, these spectral fears,
These devious dreams in which we go astray,
Dark feuds, dim sieges, toilings never done,
The febrile days, the paralytic years,
To open temperate eyes upon the sun
And rise with limbs of some more thrilling clay.

So Is It

So is it here on earth:
We serve transcendent ends
Blindly; our deed transcends
These shows and brings to birth
Effects beyond our dearth.

So is it among men:
Our iron circumstance,
Weakness, and the advance
Of hours that bring again
Frustration and mischance;

And yet these strivings blind,
This travail and this pain,
Are tissue of some brain,
The cell-work of a Mind
That waxes as we wane.

Our blind toils are the cells
That build a higher being
To see beyond our seeing,
And in our bondage dwells
A virtue for our freeing.

Homage
To T. N. W., 1942

To those who offer themselves willingly in the day
    of decision,
In the great arbitrament,
Who are prompt at the gate,
And who present themselves foremost at the fords
    of Megiddo,
And take their stations at the narrow issues:
Theirs are the great jeopardies, the necessary role,
    the memorable name,
Their encounter is with the heart of darkness.
For some the searchings of heart, the scruple,
    the fastidious witness,
For others the fateful evasion, the abiding reproaches,
For many the frivolous and the usual occasions.
But these on the crumbling levees match themselves
    with the infuriate flood.
These beneath the waves toil at the primeval sea-walls
Whose courses were laid against chaos.
These repair the moles erected of old against the
    ravining deep.
These descend where the nethermost piers of history
    are building,
And place their lives if need be at the foundation of all the
    ages of glory to come.

The Eternal Patience
Il Lago d'Orta

He guards it all in peace, this bosom of life,
This nest of nature keeps its constant sleep,
These mountain arms are patient round our strife.

Just so, a thousand years, these shadows creep
From bay to bay, oblivious of our wrong,
Just so from cloud to cloud the colors leap.

The heavens are faithful and the hills are strong,
The clouds return, and these deep seas remain,
Upon the slopes the woods forever throng.

To assault such bars of faithfulness is vain.
Our feuds surrender to these august faiths.
Beneath His lights our frantic torches wane.

His arms are round our tumults and our deaths,
His breath it is that stills our restless breaths.

Prayer Without Words

Say not a word, be still, and fear to pray;
    Forego not the great prayer of silence; plead
With the great plea of helplessness, and say
    No word but vast dependence for thy creed.

This impotence is thy best title; this
    Ebb of the spirit calls to all the seas.
The eternal travelling waters of the abyss
    And of the height know all their estuaries.

This is the last resort, the ultimate claim,
    The plea that cannot fail when all has failed.
The heart whose prayers are mocked, that in the flame
    Itself is charred or shivered, here is healed.

To Pulpit and Tribune

Speak holy words—too many blasphemies,
Too many insolent and strident cries
And jeers and taunts and maledictions rise.

Speak faithful words—too many tongues that please,
And idle vows and disingenuous pleas,
And heartless and disheartening levities.

Speak quiet words—the constellations wait,
The mountains watch; the hour for man is late
Likewise to still his heart and supplicate.

Speak chastened words—for anguish is at hand,
Intolerable, that none can understand,
And writs of ill no mortal eye has scanned.

Speak gentle words—for fallen on the knives
These sentient hearts and these exceeded lives
Bleed till their pitying Advocate arrives.

Speak holy words—and O Thou tarrying Lord,
Leave not Thy cherished to the power of the sword;
Come with Thy hosts and rout the opprobrious horde.

To the God of Deliverances

Thou who art far greater than ever we have
   explored Thee,
Whose ways far outrun our query,
Whose thoughts are deeper than Hell,
Whose devices are unimaginable
To compose our chaos,
To resolve this discord
And to lead out unsurmised gain from this our capitulation
(For we are but turbulent dreamers,
Larvae on the first steps of being).

Thou who dost yet perfect that which concerneth us
And move us, unwilling, whither our deepest will aspires;

Thou whom our truest conceptions so diminish,
Whom our most daring intimacy so finds yet so removes,
Sierra of the soul.

O Thou who remainest silent,
Whose heaven is as brass
When continents in sanguinary delirium blaspheme
   against Thee;
Yet shall not God avenge His own elect which cry day
   and night unto Him?
Yea, I tell you, He will avenge them speedily.

And thinkest thou that the Almighty made this great
   scheme of things for naught!

For that silence withers all blasphemy,
Withers all sophistry and craft of men;
Against that court of silence every lie falters in terror.

Thou who remainest silent,
Thine answers being so swift
That speech were far too tardy for Thy vindication.

O Thou who art far greater than we know Thee,
Prayer unto Thee! We thirst!

Prayer to those with thee enheavened
There where the wings of the soul beat less vainly—
Pity for the sons of men,
For these that smoulder in the long ecstacy, the long
    torment of consciousness,
Unconscious of Thee,
Burning, burning, burning.

Pity on these Thy little people,
On these who amid the darling possessions of the meek,
The tiny and fragile paradises of the poor,
Know only the brutalities of chance,
The mattock of that boor, Fortune,
The violations of the proud.

Pity for changing mortality,
The vain generations
Below the horizons of Golgotha.

It was not Thy will that man should come to naught.

O Soul of man,
Breathe life through all the members
From Thine eternal life within.
Nay, stand forth among us!
Pass once more through these shades that Thou
    has cast forth
That they may know their nature and now at last awake.

Alive for Evermore

Whom God raised up, having loosed the pangs
of death: because it was not possible that he should
be holden of it. (Acts 2:24)

His spirit lives; he died and is alive,
That pure will haunts this guilty world forever.
How could men's idle fury drive
That mighty Shepherd from his sheep? Or sever
His heart from Mary's, Peter's? Or deprive
Iscariot and the thief of his blest rod
Far in the ultimate night apart from God?
Never, never
Could death's thin shadows dim that ardent Sun!
He walks amid the Golden Candlesticks
Today, and lights all souls while time shall run
Whose troth, maintained through midnight and eclipse,
Has knit the life of God and man forever.

Unshriven

They have not known the quiet we have won,
The silence we have entered into here
Through all the exiles of this many a year,
The insensate cares that led us hither and yon.
They have not known the pardon that has fallen
Upon us from the wronged, magnanimous past,
The plenary indulgence that at last
Composed these hearts that long were vexed and sullen.
They have not known the peace that we have known—
Therefore forgive their folly and their rage,
The strange obsessive fevers of the age;
The love we know, alas, they have foregone.
They have not known the quiet we have won
Nor seen the Face that we have looked upon.

The New Aphrodite

*There is an old Celtic prophecy to the effect that the
Messiah will appear in the form of a woman at the island
of Iona to usher in the Millenium.*

How art thou wooed, thou sister of the Fair,
Thou other Aphrodite whom men ne'er
By Paphos or Valhalla's marble stair
  Looked on appalled?
  How art thou called?

Unborn! Unborn! Sister of Christ arise;
Start from the wave of Europe's tragedies
Or justify Iona's prophecies.
  Columba's isle
  Awaits thy smile.

Messiah-maid, messiah-mother, when,
When shalt thou bring thy gentler regimen,
Set thy mild ban upon the sons of men
  And mollify
  Our cruelty?

What drama of redemption is thy part?
What basenesses of ours will break thy heart,
And which of our Sanhedrin cause thy smart?
  What Calvary
  Shall we pass by?

How art thou woo'ed? How shall we lead thee home?
Daughter of Thetis and the ocean foam;
Eve unbeguiled, sister of Adam, come!
  Our evil dream
  At length redeem.

Logos

The signature of mind is on the deep
And thought has sunk its seal upon the inane,
Far fulgurations visited our sleep
And flashes lightened o'er the night's domain.
Eternity shall hold the print of dreams:
Their subtle webs and filaments shall lie
Frozen in breathless climates in the seams
Of nature like some lost fern's gossamer die.
Form in the adamantine bastions, form!
Form in the crystal sphere, the triple bronze,
Form out of naught, to outlive with type and norm
Time's crawling insect-hill that slaves and spawns.
The soul is stamped on some Atlantean range
And silence chambers it above all change.